ADVENT *GOSPEL* REFLECTIONS
JOURNAL

BISHOP ROBERT BARRON
with reflection questions by Peggy Pandaleon

WORD
on FIRE

WORD ON FIRE CATHOLIC MINISTRIES
www.WORDONFIRE.org

✠

INTRODUCTION

Friends,

Welcome to this great Advent journey! I'm so glad you're joining me and thousands of others in prayer and reflection during this holy season.

Every Advent, Christians sing a haunting song whose words go back to the ninth century. But I wonder how carefully we listen to the lyrics:

O come, O come, Emmanuel,
and ransom captive Israel
that mourns in lonely exile here
until the Son of God appears.

In the ancient world, people were tremendously afraid of being kidnapped and held for ransom. Alone, far from home, malnourished, often tortured, hostages could only hope against hope that their deliverance might come. This is the situation evoked by that well-known song: Israel, the people of God, are held for ransom in their lonely exile, and they cry out for their savior, the Son of God.

To be caught in the nexus of sin is to know the truth and to feel the texture of this imprisonment. We mourn over the sins and moral failures of our leaders; we feel trapped by our own falls into dysfunction and addiction; we feel overwhelmed by the dark powers of the world.

But the good news of Christianity is that *Emmanuel* ("God with us") has indeed appeared, and he has gone right to the bottom of sin in order to defeat it. In his full humanity, Jesus entered into that complex web of sin, and in his full divinity, he did something about it.

May we spend these holy days together in prayer, penance, and hope, fixing our eyes on the appearance of Christ our Savior and longing for his deliverance.

Peace,

+ Robert Barron

Bishop Robert Barron

ADVENT *GOSPEL* REFLECTIONS
JOURNAL

Sunday, December 2, 2018

First Sunday of Advent

LUKE 21:25-28, 34-36

Jesus said to his disciples: "There will be signs in the sun, the moon, and the stars, and on earth nations will be in dismay, perplexed by the roaring of the sea and the waves. People will die of fright in anticipation of what is coming upon the world, for the powers of the heavens will be shaken. And then they will see the Son of Man coming in a cloud with power and great glory. But when these signs begin to happen, stand erect and raise your heads because your redemption is at hand.

"Beware that your hearts do not become drowsy from carousing and drunkenness and the anxieties of daily life, and that day catch you by surprise like a trap. For that day will assault everyone who lives on the face of the earth. Be vigilant at all times and pray that you have the strength to escape the tribulations that are imminent and to stand before the Son of Man."

Friends, in today's Gospel Jesus tells his disciples to be vigilant. Today marks the beginning of Advent, the great liturgical season of vigilance, of waiting, and watching.

What practically can we do during this season of vigil keeping? What are some practices that might incarnate for us the Advent spirituality?

I strongly recommend the classically Catholic discipline of Eucharistic adoration. To spend a half hour or an hour in the presence of the Lord is not to accomplish or achieve very much—it is not really "getting" anywhere—but it is a particularly rich form of spiritual waiting.

As you keep vigil before the Blessed Sacrament, bring to Christ some problem or dilemma that you have been fretting over, and then say: "Lord, I'm waiting for you to solve this, to show me the way out, the way forward. I've been running, planning, worrying, but now I'm going to let you work." Then, throughout Advent, watch attentively for signs.

Also, when you pray before the Eucharist, allow your desire for the things of God to intensify; allow your heart and soul to expand. Pray, "Lord, make me ready to receive the gifts you want to give," or even, "Lord Jesus, surprise me."

Reflect When you are before the Eucharist in adoration, what will you ask the Lord to do for you this Advent?

_____

_____

_____

_____

_____

_____

_____

_____

_____

_____

_____

_____

_____

_____

Monday, December 3, 2018

Memorial of Saint Francis Xavier, Priest

MATTHEW 8:5-11

When Jesus entered Capernaum, a centurion approached him and appealed to him, saying, "Lord, my servant is lying at home paralyzed, suffering dreadfully." He said to him, "I will come and cure him." The centurion said in reply, "Lord, I am not worthy to have you enter under my roof; only say the word and my servant will be healed. For I too am a man subject to authority, with soldiers subject to me. And I say to one, 'Go,' and he goes; and to another, 'Come here,' and he comes; and to my slave, 'Do this,' and he does it." When Jesus heard this, he was amazed and said to those following him, "Amen, I say to you, in no one in Israel have I found such faith. I say to you, many will come from the east and the west, and will recline with Abraham, Isaac, and Jacob at the banquet in the Kingdom of heaven."

Friends, today's Gospel passage acclaims a centurion's trust in the Lord Jesus. To trust is to have hope, to turn one's heart to God. It means to root one's life, to ground and center one's concerns in God. And, oppositely, to trust and to turn one's heart to human beings means to root the whole of one's life, to ground and center one's concerns, in the things of this world, in wealth, fame, power, honor, or pleasure.

What is the center of gravity of your life? What is your "ultimate concern"? The Bible consistently lays this out as an either/or. Think of the passage in the book of Joshua, when Joshua lays it on the line for the people of Israel: "Do you serve the Lord or some other gods?"

Jesus tells his followers, "Either you are with me or you are against me." Today's Gospel reminds us that we each have to answer this question with great honesty and clarity.

Reflect   What desires or plans have crowded Jesus out of the center of your life?

Tuesday, December 4, 2018
LUKE 21:25-28, 34-36

Jesus rejoiced in the Holy Spirit and said, "I give you praise, Father, Lord of heaven and earth, for although you have hidden these things from the wise and the learned you have revealed them to the childlike. Yes, Father, such has been your gracious will. All things have been handed over to me by my Father. No one knows who the Son is except the Father, and who the Father is except the Son and anyone to whom the Son wishes to reveal him."

Turning to the disciples in private he said, "Blessed are the eyes that see what you see. For I say to you, many prophets and kings desired to see what you see, but did not see it, and to hear what you hear, but did not hear it."

Friends, today in the Gospel we hear Jesus in intimate conversation with his Father. The passage invites us into very deep mysteries. Jesus addresses his Father and thereby reveals his own deepest identity within the Holy Trinity. He says, "I praise you, Father, Lord of heaven and earth, for although you have hidden these things from the wise and learned, you have revealed them to the little ones."

It is important to keep in mind that this is not simply a good and holy man addressing God, but rather the very Son of God addressing his Father. We are being given a share in the inner life of God, the conversation between the first two Trinitarian persons.

And what are the "things" that have been concealed from the learned and revealed to the little ones? Nothing other than the mystery of Jesus' relationship to his Father, the love that obtains between Father and Son, the inner life of God. From the beginning, this is what God wanted to give us.

Reflect   How is the love that God gives us different from human love?

_____

_____

_____

_____

_____

_____

_____

_____

_____

_____

_____

_____

_____

_____

_____

_____

_____

_____

_____

_____

Wednesday, December 5, 2018

MATTHEW 15:29-37

At that time: Jesus walked by the Sea of Galilee, went up on the mountain, and sat down there. Great crowds came to him, having with them the lame, the blind, the deformed, the mute, and many others. They placed them at his feet, and he cured them. The crowds were amazed when they saw the mute speaking, the deformed made whole, the lame walking, and the blind able to see, and they glorified the God of Israel.

Jesus summoned his disciples and said, "My heart is moved with pity for the crowd, for they have been with me now for three days and have nothing to eat. I do not want to send them away hungry, for fear they may collapse on the way." The disciples said to him, "Where could we ever get enough bread in this deserted place to satisfy such a crowd?" Jesus said to them, "How many loaves do you have?" "Seven," they replied, "and a few fish." He ordered the crowd to sit down on the ground. Then he took the seven loaves and the fish, gave thanks, broke the loaves, and gave them to the disciples, who in turn gave them to the crowds. They all ate and were satisfied. They picked up the fragments left over—seven baskets full.

Friends, our Gospel today tells about the feeding of the four thousand. Jesus instructs the crowd to sit on the ground. Taking the seven loaves and a few fish, Jesus makes a meal that satisfies the enormous crowd. They are hungry, tired, and worn out from their exertions, and Jesus gives them sustenance for the day.

For Thomas Aquinas, the great metaphor for the Eucharist is sustenance, food for the journey. The Eucharist is daily food, sustenance for the journey, nourishment to get us through the day-to-day. How effective would we be if we never ate, or ate only on special occasions and in a festive environment? Not very. So, in the spiritual life, we must eat and drink or we will not have strength.

Is this just meant in some vague symbolic way? No, rather in a vividly analogical way. For just as the body needs physical nourishment, the spirit needs spiritual nourishment, and there is no getting around this law.

Sometimes we think it's no big deal if we stay away from Mass and refrain from receiving Communion. Think again!

Reflect   During a typical week, how do you get spiritual nourishment? Is it enough?

_____

_____

_____

_____

_____

_____

_____

_____

_____

_____

_____

_____

_____

_____

Thursday, December 6, 2018

MATTHEW 7:21, 24-27

*J*esus said to his disciples: *"Not everyone who says to me, 'Lord, Lord,' will enter the Kingdom of heaven, but only the one who does the will of my Father in heaven.*

"Everyone who listens to these words of mine and acts on them will be like a wise man who built his house on rock. The rain fell, the floods came, and the winds blew and buffeted the house. But it did not collapse; it had been set solidly on rock. And everyone who listens to these words of mine but does not act on them will be like a fool who built his house on sand. The rain fell, the floods came, and the winds blew and buffeted the house. And it collapsed and was completely ruined."

Friends, today's Gospel asks how we apply the Lord's teaching. "Everyone who listens to these words of mine and acts on them will be like a wise man who built his house on rock. The rain fell, the floods came, and the winds blew and buffeted the house. But it did not collapse." This is the heart of it: if you are rooted in God, then you can withstand anything, precisely because you are linked to that power which is creating the cosmos. You will be blessed at the deepest place, and nothing can finally touch you.

But the one who does not take Jesus' words to heart "will be like the fool who built his house on sand. The rain fell, the floods came, and the winds buffeted the house. And it collapsed and was completely ruined." When the inevitable trials come, the life built on pleasure, money, power, or fame will give way.

So the question is a simple one: Where do you stand? How goes it with your heart? On what, precisely, is the whole of your life built?

Reflect How do you "build your house on rock" or become "rooted in God"?

_____

_____

_____

_____

_____

_____

_____

_____

_____

_____

_____

_____

_____

_____

_____

_____

_____

_____

_____

_____

_____

_____

Friday, December 7, 2018

Memorial of St. Ambrose, Bishop & Doctor of the Church

MATTHEW 9:27-31

As Jesus passed by, two blind men followed him, crying out, "Son of David, have pity on us!" When he entered the house, the blind men approached him and Jesus said to them, "Do you believe that I can do this?" "Yes, Lord," they said to him. Then he touched their eyes and said, "Let it be done for you according to your faith." And their eyes were opened. Jesus warned them sternly, "See that no one knows about this." But they went out and spread word of him through all that land.

Friends, today's Gospel passage celebrates the faith of two blind men. To have faith is—to use the current jargon—to live outside the box, risking, venturing, believing the impossible. When we remain in the narrow confines of our perceptions, our thoughts, or our hopes, we live in a very cramped way. We become closed off to the possibility that sometimes, the power of faith is manifested in spectacular and immediately obvious ways. When someone consciously and confidently opens himself to God, acting as a kind of conduit, the divine energy can flow.

Faith allows someone to live in detachment from all of the ups and downs of life. In the language of St. Ignatius of Loyola: "Lord, I don't care whether I have a long life or a short life, whether I am rich or poor, whether I am healthy or sick." Someone that lives in that kind of detachment is free, and because they are free, they are powerful. They are beyond the threats that arise in the context of this world. This is the source of *dynamis*, of real power.

Reflect How detached are you from the ups and downs of life? What prevents you from being more detached?

Saturday, December 8, 2018
Solemnity *of the* Immaculate Conception
of the Blessed Virgin Mary

LUKE 1:26-38

The angel Gabriel was sent from God to a town of Galilee called Nazareth, to a virgin betrothed to a man named Joseph, of the house of David, and the virgin's name was Mary. And coming to her, he said, "Hail, full of grace! The Lord is with you." But she was greatly troubled at what was said and pondered what sort of greeting this might be. Then the angel said to her, "Do not be afraid, Mary, for you have found favor with God. Behold, you will conceive in your womb and bear a son, and you shall name him Jesus. He will be great and will be called Son of the Most High, and the Lord God will give him the throne of David his father, and he will rule over the house of Jacob forever, and of his Kingdom there will be no end." But Mary said to the angel, "How can this be, since I have no relations with a man?" And the angel said to her in reply, "The Holy Spirit will come upon you, and the power of the Most High will overshadow you. Therefore the child to be born will be called holy, the Son of God. And behold, Elizabeth, your relative, has also conceived a son in her old age, and this is the sixth month for her who was called barren; for nothing will be impossible for God." Mary said, "Behold, I am the handmaid of the Lord. May it be done to me according to your word." Then the angel departed from her.

Friends, today we celebrate the feast of the Immaculate Conception. The Church Fathers consistently referred to Mary as the New Eve, which is to say, the one who reversed the momentum started by the mother of the human race. The *Ave* of the angel was seen as the reversal of *Eva*. While Eve grasped at divinity, Mary said, "Let it be done unto me."

Here's the liberating paradox: passivity before objective values is precisely what makes life wonderful. Allowing oneself to be invaded and rearranged by objective value is what makes life worth living. And this applies unsurpassably to our relationship with God. The message that your life is not about you does indeed crush the false self that would bend the whole world to its purposes, but it sets free the true self.

The Immaculate Conception itself is concealed in the privacy of salvation history, but the effects of it are on clear display in this Gospel. In the presence of the supreme value, we ought to say, along with Mary, "Be it done unto me!"

Reflect When have you said to God, "Let it be done unto me"? When *should* you have said it?

Sunday, December 9, 2018

Second Sunday of Advent

LUKE 3:1-6

In the fifteenth year of the reign of Tiberius Caesar, when Pontius Pilate was governor of Judea, and Herod was tetrarch of Galilee, and his brother Philip tetrarch of the region of Ituraea and Trachonitis, and Lysanias was tetrarch of Abilene, during the high priesthood of Annas and Caiaphas, the word of God came to John the son of Zechariah in the desert. John went throughout the whole region of the Jordan, proclaiming a baptism of repentance for the forgiveness of sins, as it is written in the book of the words of the prophet Isaiah:

A voice of one crying out in the desert:
Prepare the way of the Lord,
make straight his paths.
Every valley shall be filled
and every mountain and hill shall be made low.
The winding roads shall be made straight,
and the rough ways made smooth,
and all flesh shall see the salvation of God.

Friends, in today's Gospel Luke quotes from the prophet Isaiah: "Prepare the way of the Lord, make straight his paths."

Advent is a great liturgical season of waiting—but not a passive waiting. We yearn, we search, and we reach out for the God who will come to us in human flesh. In short, we prepare the way of the Lord Jesus Christ.

This preparation has a penitential dimension, because the season in which we prepare for the coming of a savior, and we don't need a savior unless we're deeply convinced there is something to be saved from. When we have become deeply aware of our sin, we know that we can cling to nothing in ourselves, that everything we offer is, to some degree, tainted and impure. We can't show our cultural, professional, and personal accomplishments to God as though they are enough to save us. But the moment we realize that fact, we move into the Advent spirit, desperately craving a savior.

In the book of Isaiah, we read: "Yet, O Lord, you are our father; we are the clay and you are the potter: we are all the work of your hands." Today, let us prepare ourselves for the potter to come.

Reflect When you have "yearned, searched, or reached out" for God? Is it only when you couldn't handle things yourself, or is it more often?

_____

_____

_____

_____

_____

_____

_____

_____

_____

_____

_____

_____

_____

Monday, December 10, 2018

LUKE 5:17-26

One day as Jesus was teaching, Pharisees and teachers of the law, who had come from every village of Galilee and Judea and Jerusalem, were sitting there, and the power of the Lord was with him for healing. And some men brought on a stretcher a man who was paralyzed; they were trying to bring him in and set him in his presence. But not finding a way to bring him in because of the crowd, they went up on the roof and lowered him on the stretcher through the tiles into the middle in front of Jesus. When Jesus saw their faith, he said, "As for you, your sins are forgiven."

Then the scribes and Pharisees began to ask themselves, "Who is this who speaks blasphemies? Who but God alone can forgive sins?" Jesus knew their thoughts and said to them in reply, "What are you thinking in your hearts? Which is easier, to say, 'Your sins are forgiven,' or to say, 'Rise and walk'? But that you may know that the Son of Man has authority on earth to forgive sins"—he said to the one who was paralyzed, "I say to you, rise, pick up your stretcher, and go home."

He stood up immediately before them, picked up what he had been lying on, and went home, glorifying God. Then astonishment seized them all and they glorified God, and, struck with awe, they said, "We have seen incredible things today."

Friends, our Gospel for today tells that wonderful story of the healing of the paralytic. People gather by the dozens to hear Jesus, crowding around the doorway of the house. They bring him a paralyzed man, and because there is no way to get him through the door, they climb up on the roof and open a space to lower him down.

Can I suggest a connection between this wonderful narrative and our present evangelical situation? There are an awful lot of Catholics who are paralyzed, unable to move, frozen in regard to Christ and the Church.

This might be from doubt, from fear, from anger, from old resentment, from ignorance, or from self-reproach. Some of these reasons might be good; some might be bad.

Your job, as a believer, is to bring others to Christ. How? A word of encouragement, a challenge, an explanation, a word of forgiveness, a note, a phone call. We notice the wonderful urgency of these people as they bring the sick man to Jesus. Do we feel the same urgency within his Mystical Body today?

Reflect Who do you urgently want to bring to Christ? How can you take the next step?

Tuesday, December 11, 2018

MATTHEW 18:12-14

*J*esus said to his disciples: *"What is your opinion? If a man has a hundred sheep and one of them goes astray, will he not leave the ninety-nine in the hills and go in search of the stray? And if he finds it, amen, I say to you, he rejoices more over it than over the ninety-nine that did not stray. In just the same way, it is not the will of your heavenly Father that one of these little ones be lost."*

Friends, today's Gospel passage recounts the story of the shepherd finding his lost sheep. Let's look at that lost sheep. A sheep is something more than a lost coin—which is to say, it has mobility, sense, appetites, and so on. Many years ago, when I was on retreat at the Abbey of Tamie in the Alps, I heard the desperate bleating of a sheep who had fallen into a pit. All night he cried, knowing that he was in trouble and hoping that someone would come to save him.

There are souls who are like the lost sheep. Spiritually compromised, fundamentally unable to help themselves, they are at least aware that they are in a mess. They are like people who commence the AA process by admitting that they have hit bottom and are out of control. They bleat, they cry for help.

And God finds them—and when he finds them, he carries them back, for they are unable to move on their own.

Reflect When has God "found you and carried you back" in your own life?

_____

_____

_____

_____

_____

_____

_____

_____

_____

_____

_____

_____

_____

_____

_____

_____

_____

_____

_____

_____

*M*ary set out and traveled to the hill country in haste to a town of Judah, where she entered the house of Zechariah and greeted Elizabeth. When Elizabeth heard Mary's greeting, the infant leaped in her womb, and Elizabeth, filled with the Holy Spirit, cried out in a loud voice and said, "Most blessed are you among women, and blessed is the fruit of your womb. And how does this happen to me, that the mother of my Lord should come to me? For at the moment the sound of your greeting reached my ears, the infant in my womb leaped for joy. Blessed are you who believed that what was spoken to you by the Lord would be fulfilled."

And Mary said:

"My soul proclaims the greatness of the Lord;
my spirit rejoices in God my savior."

Friends, today we celebrate the great feast of Our Lady of Guadalupe. What followed the apparition of Mary at Tepeyac is one of the most astounding chapters in the history of Christian evangelism.

Though Franciscan missionaries had been laboring in Mexico for twenty years, they had made little progress. But within ten years of the appearance of Our Lady of Guadalupe practically the entire Mexican people, nine million strong, had converted to Christianity. *La Morena* had proved a more effective evangelist than Peter, Paul, St. Patrick, and St. Francis Xavier combined! And with that great national conversion, the Aztec practice of human sacrifice came to an end. She had done battle with fallen spirits and had won a culture-changing victory for the God of love.

The challenge for us who honor her today is to join the same fight. We must announce to our culture today the truth of the God of Israel, the

God of Jesus Christ, the God of nonviolence and forgiving love. And we ought, like *La Morena,* to be bearers of Jesus to a world that needs him more than ever.

Reflect Following Mary's example, how can you be a "bearer of Christ" to your own family and community?

_____

_____

_____

_____

_____

_____

_____

_____

_____

_____

_____

_____

_____

_____

_____

_____

_____

_____

_____

Thursday, December 13, 2018

Memorial of Saint Lucy, Virgin and Martyr

MATTHEW 11:11-15

> *esus said to the crowds: "Amen, I say to you, among those born of women there has been none greater than John the Baptist; yet the least in the Kingdom of heaven is greater than he. From the days of John the Baptist until now, the Kingdom of heaven suffers violence, and the violent are taking it by force. All the prophets and the law prophesied up to the time of John. And if you are willing to accept it, he is Elijah, the one who is to come. Whoever has ears ought to hear."*

Friends, in today's Gospel Jesus says to the crowds: "From the days of John the Baptist until now, the Kingdom of heaven suffers violence, and the violent are taking it by force."

The name of Flannery O'Connor's second novel was taken from the Douay-Rheims translation of this last line: "the violent bear it away." What do we make of this strange and famously ambiguous wording?

Many have taken it to mean that the kingdom of God is attacked by violent people, such as those who killed John the Baptist, and that they threaten to take it away. But others have interpreted it in the opposite direction, as a word of praise to the spiritually violent who manage to get into the kingdom. O'Connor herself sides with this latter group. In one of her letters, she says, "St. Thomas' gloss on this verse is that the violent Christ is here talking about represent those ascetics who strain against mere nature. St. Augustine concurs."

The "mere nature" that classical Christianity describes is a fallen nature, one that tends away from God and his demands. The "violent," on this reading, are those spiritually heroic types who resist the promptings and tendencies of this nature and seek to discipline it in order to enter into the kingdom of God.

Reflect In what ways have you disciplined your own sinful nature to draw closer to the kingdom of God?

Friday, December 14, 2018
Memorial of Saint John of the Cross,
Priest and Doctor of the Church
MATTHEW 11:16-19

Jesus said to the crowds: "To what shall I compare this generation? It is like children who sit in marketplaces and call to one another, 'We played the flute for you, but you did not dance, we sang a dirge but you did not mourn.' For John came neither eating nor drinking, and they said, 'He is possessed by a demon.' The Son of Man came eating and drinking and they said, 'Look, he is a glutton and a drunkard, a friend of tax collectors and sinners.' But wisdom is vindicated by her works."

Friends, in today's Gospel the Pharisees compare the eating habits of John the Baptist, who fasted, and Jesus, who dined with sinners. In the carefully stratified society of Jesus' time, a righteous person would never associate with the unrighteous, for fear of becoming unclean.

But here is Jesus, scandalizing everyone because he does indeed break down these barriers. How would you feel if you saw me socializing with prostitutes and drug-dealers, eating and drinking with terrorists? Would it shock you, dismay you, disappoint you? But this is what Jesus did, precisely because he was the incarnation of the God who aggressively seeks out the lost.

God looks for us, comes running after us, never lets go, never relents, never gives up. The more we run, the more he runs after; the more we hide, the more he looks; the more we resist, the more he persists. God loves sinners and associates with them.

Reflect   Name someone you know whom you consider "lost." How can you reach out to this person before Advent ends, following Jesus' command to "love your neighbor"?

Saturday, December 15, 2018

MATTHEW 17:9A, 10-13

As they were coming down from the mountain, the disciples asked Jesus, "Why do the scribes say that Elijah must come first?" He said in reply, "Elijah will indeed come and restore all things; but I tell you that Elijah has already come, and they did not recognize him but did to him whatever they pleased. So also will the Son of Man suffer at their hands." Then the disciples understood that he was speaking to them of John the Baptist.

Friends, today's Gospel passage identifies the appearance of John the Baptist with the expected return of the prophet Elijah. John, the herald of Christ, appears in the desert. Here he stands for all of us in the desert of sin, the lifeless place. It is as though John purposely went there to remind us of our need for grace.

What is he proclaiming? A baptism of repentance. This is the great message. Turn your life over to a higher power. People are coming to him from all sides, because in our heart of hearts we all resonate with this message.

So often in the Old Testament the prophets are asked to act out some quality of the people, perhaps something they were unable or unwilling to see. Well, this tradition continues here: John acts out for the people their helplessness and neediness before the Lord. But then, like Isaiah, he refuses to leave it at that. He announces that one is coming, one who will baptize in the Holy Spirit.

Reflect About what pattern of sinful behavior do you feel helpless and most in need of a savior to remedy?

_____

_____

_____

_____

_____

_____

_____

_____

_____

_____

_____

_____

_____

_____

_____

_____

_____

_____

_____

_____

_____

Sunday, December 16, 2018

Third Sunday *of* Advent

LUKE 3:10-18

The crowds asked John the Baptist, "What should we do?" He said to them in reply, "Whoever has two cloaks should share with the person who has none. And whoever has food should do likewise." Even tax collectors came to be baptized and they said to him, "Teacher, what should we do?" He answered them, "Stop collecting more than what is prescribed." Soldiers also asked him, "And what is it that we should do?" He told them, "Do not practice extortion, do not falsely accuse anyone, and be satisfied with your wages."

Now the people were filled with expectation, and all were asking in their hearts whether John might be the Christ. John answered them all, saying, "I am baptizing you with water, but one mightier than I is coming. I am not worthy to loosen the thongs of his sandals. He will baptize you with the Holy Spirit and fire. His winnowing fan is in his hand to clear his threshing floor and to gather the wheat into his barn, but the chaff he will burn with unquenchable fire." Exhorting them in many other ways, he preached good news to the people.

Friends, like those in the time of John the Baptist, we ask: "What should we do?" How should we live our lives?

This question, of course, tells us something else about repentance: that it has to do with action more than simply changing our minds. The spiritual life is, finally, a set of behaviors.

So what does John the Baptist tell us to do? His first recommendation is this: "Whoever has two cloaks should share with the person who has none." This is so basic, so elemental—yet so almost thoroughly ignored! In the Church's social teaching, we find a constant reminder that although private property is a social good, the use of our private property must always have a social orientation.

An early Church Father, St. Basil the Great, expressed the idea in tones that echo John the Baptist: "The bread in your cupboard belongs to the hungry. The cloak in your wardrobe belongs to the naked. The shoes you allow to rot belong to the barefoot. The money in your vaults belongs to the destitute. You do injustice to every man whom you could help but do not."

So what should we do this Advent, we who seek repentance, we who await the coming of the Messiah? Serve justice, render to each his due, and give to those who are in need.

Reflect What did you give to someone in need last week?

Monday, December 17, 2018

MATTHEW 1:1-17

*T*he book of the genealogy of Jesus Christ,
the son of David, the son of Abraham.

Abraham became the father of Isaac,
Isaac the father of Jacob,
Jacob the father of Judah and his brothers.
Judah became the father of Perez and Zerah,
whose mother was Tamar.
Perez became the father of Hezron,
Hezron the father of Ram,
Ram the father of Amminadab.
Amminadab became the father of Nahshon,
Nahshon the father of Salmon,
Salmon the father of Boaz,
whose mother was Rahab.
Boaz became the father of Obed,
whose mother was Ruth.
Obed became the father of Jesse,
Jesse the father of David the king.

David became the father of Solomon,
whose mother had been the wife of Uriah.
Solomon became the father of Rehoboam,
Rehoboam the father of Abijah,
Abijah the father of Asaph.
Asaph became the father of Jehoshaphat,
Jehoshaphat the father of Joram,
Joram the father of Uzziah.
Uzziah became the father of Jotham,
Jotham the father of Ahaz,
Ahaz the father of Hezekiah.
Hezekiah became the father of Manasseh,

Manasseh the father of Amos,
Amos the father of Josiah.
Josiah became the father of Jechoniah and his brothers
at the time of the Babylonian exile.

After the Babylonian exile,
Jechoniah became the father of Shealtiel,
Shealtiel the father of Zerubbabel,
Zerubbabel the father of Abiud.
Abiud became the father of Eliakim,
Eliakim the father of Azor,
Azor the father of Zadok.
Zadok became the father of Achim,
Achim the father of Eliud,
Eliud the father of Eleazar.
Eleazar became the father of Matthan,
Matthan the father of Jacob,
Jacob the father of Joseph, the husband of Mary.
Of her was born Jesus who is called the Christ.

Thus the total number of generations
from Abraham to David
is fourteen generations;
from David to the Babylonian exile, fourteen generations;
from the Babylonian exile to the Christ,
fourteen generations.

Friends, today's Gospel records the genealogy of Jesus. It was desperately important for Matthew to show that Jesus didn't just appear out of the blue. Rather, he came out of a rich, densely textured history. St. Irenaeus tells us that the Incarnation had been taking place over a long period of time, with God gradually accustoming himself to the human race.

Look at this long line of characters: saints, sinners, cheats, prostitutes, murderers, poets, kings, insiders, and outsiders—all leading to the

Christ. Of course, King David is mentioned. He was, without doubt, a great figure, the king who united the nation. But he was also an adulterer and a murderer.

From this long line of the great and not-so-great, the prominent and obscure, saints and sinners, and kings and paupers came "Jesus who is called the Messiah." God became one of us, in all of our grace and embarrassment, in all of our beauty and ordinariness. God had a series of human ancestors, and, like most families, they were kind of a mixed bag. And what good news this is for us! It means that God can bring the Christ to birth even in people like us.

Reflect What ancestors or family members have helped Christ be born in you? How was he born in you despite less helpful relatives you may have?

_____

_____

_____

_____

_____

_____

_____

_____

_____

_____

_____

_____

_____

Tuesday, December 18, 2018

MATTHEW 1:18-25

*T*his is how the birth of Jesus Christ came about. When his mother Mary was betrothed to Joseph, but before they lived together, she was found with child through the Holy Spirit. Joseph her husband, since he was a righteous man, yet unwilling to expose her to shame, decided to divorce her quietly. Such was his intention when, behold, the angel of the Lord appeared to him in a dream and said, "Joseph, son of David, do not be afraid to take Mary your wife into your home. For it is through the Holy Spirit that this child has been conceived in her. She will bear a son and you are to name him Jesus, because he will save his people from their sins." All this took place to fulfill what the Lord had said through the prophet:

> Behold, the virgin shall be with child and bear a son,
> and they shall name him Emmanuel,

which means "God is with us." When Joseph awoke, he did as the angel of the Lord had commanded him and took his wife into his home. He had no relations with her until she bore a son, and he named him Jesus.

Friends, today's Gospel centers on the intriguing figure of Joseph. Joseph is one of the most beloved of the saints, featured in countless works of art and prominent in the devotional lives of many.

We know almost nothing about him, yet some very powerful spiritual themes emerge in the accounts of Joseph. He had become betrothed to Mary and this union had been blessed by God. And then he finds that his betrothed is pregnant.

This must have been an emotional maelstrom for him. And, at a deeper level, it is a spiritual crisis. What does God want him to do? Then the angel appears to him in a dream and tells him, "Joseph, son of David, do not be afraid to take Mary your wife into your home." He realizes at that moment that these puzzling events are part of a much greater plan of God's. What appears to be a disaster from his perspective is meaningful from God's perspective.

Joseph was willing to cooperate with the divine plan, though he in no way knew its contours or deepest purpose. Like Mary at the Annunciation, he trusted and let himself be led.

Reflect When have you "cooperated with the divine plan" even though you did not understand it or know its entire purpose?

_____

_____

_____

_____

_____

_____

_____

_____

_____

_____

_____

_____

_____

Wednesday, December 19, 2018

LUKE 1:5-25

In the days of Herod, King of Judea, there was a priest named Zechariah of the priestly division of Abijah; his wife was from the daughters of Aaron, and her name was Elizabeth. Both were righteous in the eyes of God, observing all the commandments and ordinances of the Lord blamelessly. But they had no child, because Elizabeth was barren and both were advanced in years.

Once when he was serving as priest in his division's turn before God, according to the practice of the priestly service, he was chosen by lot to enter the sanctuary of the Lord to burn incense. Then, when the whole assembly of the people was praying outside at the hour of the incense offering, the angel of the Lord appeared to him, standing at the right of the altar of incense. Zechariah was troubled by what he saw, and fear came upon him.

But the angel said to him, "Do not be afraid, Zechariah, because your prayer has been heard. Your wife Elizabeth will bear you a son, and you shall name him John. And you will have joy and gladness, and many will rejoice at his birth, for he will be great in the sight of the Lord. He will drink neither wine nor strong drink. He will be filled with the Holy Spirit even from his mother's womb, and he will turn many of the children of Israel to the Lord their God. He will go before him in the spirit and power of Elijah to turn the hearts of fathers toward children and the disobedient to the understanding of the righteous, to prepare a people fit for the Lord."

Then Zechariah said to the angel, "How shall I know this? For I am an old man, and my wife is advanced in years." And the angel said to him in reply, "I am Gabriel, who stand before God. I was sent to speak to you and to announce to you this good news. But now you will be speechless and unable to talk until the day these things take place, because you did not believe my words, which will be fulfilled at their proper time."

Meanwhile the people were waiting for Zechariah and were amazed that he stayed so long in the sanctuary. But when he came out, he was unable to speak to them, and they realized that he had seen a vision in the sanctuary. He was gesturing to them but remained mute.

Then, when his days of ministry were completed, he went home.

After this time his wife Elizabeth conceived, and she went into seclusion for five months, saying, "So has the Lord done for me at a time when he has seen fit to take away my disgrace before others."

Friends, in today's Gospel, Luke tells us about John the Baptist's parents. We see with utter clarity that John is a priestly figure. Zechariah, his father, is a Temple priest, and Elizabeth, his mother, is a descendant of Aaron, the very first priest.

Now flash forward thirty years and see John emerging in the desert. The first question is, "Why is this son of a priest not working in the Temple?" And the second is, "Why are the people going out from Jerusalem to commune with him?" The answer to the first is that he is engaging in a prophetic critique of a Temple that has gone bad. And the answer to the second is that he is performing the acts of a purified Temple priest out in the desert. His baptism was a ritual cleansing and a spur to repent, precisely what a pious Jew would have sought in the Temple.

And the picture becomes complete when Jesus arrives to be baptized, and John says, "Behold, the Lamb of God." This is explicitly Temple talk. He is saying that the one who is to be sacrificed has arrived. He is the fulfillment of priesthood, Temple, and sacrifice. The priestly figure has done his work, and now he fades away.

Reflect What is your vocation and how do you carry it out according to God's will?

Thursday, December 20, 2018

LUKE 1:26-38

In the sixth month, the angel Gabriel was sent from God to a town of Galilee called Nazareth, to a virgin betrothed to a man named Joseph, of the house of David, and the virgin's name was Mary. And coming to her, he said, "Hail, full of grace! The Lord is with you." But she was greatly troubled at what was said and pondered what sort of greeting this might be. Then the angel said to her, "Do not be afraid, Mary, for you have found favor with God. Behold, you will conceive in your womb and bear a son, and you shall name him Jesus. He will be great and will be called Son of the Most High, and the Lord God will give him the throne of David his father, and he will rule over the house of Jacob forever, and of his Kingdom there will be no end."

But Mary said to the angel, "How can this be, since I have no relations with a man?" And the angel said to her in reply, "The Holy Spirit will come upon you, and the power of the Most High will overshadow you. Therefore the child to be born will be called holy, the Son of God. And behold, Elizabeth, your relative, has also conceived a son in her old age, and this is the sixth month for her who was called barren; for nothing will be impossible for God."

Mary said, "Behold, I am the handmaid of the Lord. May it be done to me according to your word." Then the angel departed from her.

Friends, in today's Gospel of Luke, we find the Annunciation to Mary. Here is what Gabriel said to the Virgin: "Thou shalt conceive in thy womb and bring forth a son, and shalt call his name Jesus...The Lord God shall give unto him the throne of his father David: And he shall reign over the house of Jacob forever; and of his kingdom there shall be no end."

No first-century Israelite would have missed the meaning here: this child shall be the fulfillment of the promise made to King David.

And this means that the child is, in fact, the king of the world, the one who would bring unity and peace to the nations. The conviction grew upon Israel that this mysterious descendent of David would be king—not just for a time and not just in an earthly sense, but ruling forever and for all nations. This definitive king of the Jews would be king of the world. He would be our king as well.

Reflect How does Jesus reign as king in your personal life?

Friday, December 21, 2018

LUKE 1:39-45

*M*ary set out in those days and traveled to the hill country in haste to a town of Judah, where she entered the house of Zechariah and greeted Elizabeth. When Elizabeth heard Mary's greeting, the infant leaped in her womb, and Elizabeth, filled with the Holy Spirit, cried out in a loud voice and said, "Most blessed are you among women, and blessed is the fruit of your womb. And how does this happen to me, that the mother of my Lord should come to me? For at the moment the sound of your greeting reached my ears, the infant in my womb leaped for joy. Blessed are you who believed that what was spoken to you by the Lord would be fulfilled."

Friends, today's Gospel tells of Mary's visit to Elizabeth. I've always been fascinated by Mary's "haste" in this story of the Visitation. Upon hearing the message of Gabriel concerning her own pregnancy and that of her cousin, Mary "proceeded in haste into the hill country of Judah" to see Elizabeth.

Why did she go with such speed and purpose? Because she had found her mission, her role in the theo-drama. We are dominated today by the ego-drama in all of its ramifications and implications. The ego-drama is the play that I'm writing, I'm producing, I'm directing, and I'm starring in. We see this absolutely everywhere in our culture. Freedom of choice reigns supreme; I become the person that I choose to be.

The theo-drama is the great story being told by God, the great play being directed by God. What makes life thrilling is to discover your role in it. This is precisely what has happened to Mary. She has found her role—indeed a climactic role—in the theo-drama, and she wants to conspire with Elizabeth, who has also discovered her role in the same drama. And, like Mary, we have to find our place in God's story.

Reflect   What is your place in God's story, the theo-drama? If you're not sure, what steps can you take to discern his plan for your life?

*M*ary said:

"My soul proclaims the greatness of the Lord;
my spirit rejoices in God my savior.
for he has looked upon his lowly servant.
From this day all generations will call me blessed:
the Almighty has done great things for me,
and holy is his Name.
He has mercy on those who fear him
in every generation.
He has shown the strength of his arm,
and has scattered the proud in their conceit.
He has cast down the mighty from their thrones
and has lifted up the lowly.
He has filled the hungry with good things,
and the rich he has sent away empty.
He has come to the help of his servant Israel
for he remembered his promise of mercy,
the promise he made to our fathers,
to Abraham and his children for ever."

Mary remained with Elizabeth about three months
and then returned to her home.

Friends, by far, the most important Advent figure is Mary of Nazareth, the Mother of God, for Mary sums up in her person the whole of the people Israel, the nation whose whole purpose was to prepare for the coming of the Lord. In her great *Magnificat*, which we hear in today's Gospel, Mary is the new Isaiah and the new Jeremiah and the new Ezekiel, for she announces with the greatest clarity and joy the coming of the Messiah.

What was only vaguely foreseen in those great prophetic figures is now in clear focus: "He has shown the strength of his arm; he has scattered the proud in their conceit; he has filled the hungry with good things and the rich he has sent away empty. He has come to the help of his servant Israel, for he has remembered his promise of mercy, the promise he made to our fathers, to Abraham and his children forever."

There is nothing stronger or more beautiful in any of the prophets.

Reflect Think about Mary's acceptance of Gabriel's message and her ready consent to God's plan. How does Mary model perfect faith?

Sunday, December 23, 2018

Fourth Sunday of Advent

LUKE 1:39-45

Mary set out and traveled to the hill country in haste to a town of Judah, where she entered the house of Zechariah and greeted Elizabeth. When Elizabeth heard Mary's greeting, the infant leaped in her womb, and Elizabeth, filled with the Holy Spirit, cried out in a loud voice and said, "Blessed are you among women, and blessed is the fruit of your womb. And how does this happen to me, that the mother of my Lord should come to me? For at the moment the sound of your greeting reached my ears, the infant in my womb leaped for joy. Blessed are you who believed that what was spoken to you by the Lord would be fulfilled."

Friends, in the eleventh chapter of the book of Revelation, the visionary sees in the heavenly place the Ark of the Covenant—that box in which the remnants of the Ten Commandments were kept, that sign of Yahweh's presence among his people. Immediately after, we hear of a queen who is about to give birth to a son. As a dragon waits to devour the child, the mother and child are swept away, and a great war breaks out between Michael and his angels and the enemy.

This sequence is not accidental. In today's Gospel, we see Mary as the true Ark of the Covenant. She bore in her own womb the Word made flesh and the very presence of God. When she visits her cousin Elizabeth, the infant John the Baptist leapt in his mother's womb, doing his own version of David's dance before the Ark.

But Mary, as both the true Ark and the Queen Mother of Israel, is also a fighter. Israel frequently brought the Ark into battle with them, and the king of Israel and his queen mother were warrior figures. Mary is all about spiritual warfare against powers and principalities.

This terrible crisis we're passing through in the Catholic Church has been a diabolical masterpiece. It undermines the work of the Church in practically every way. So what do we do? Get in the army of Christ the Warrior-King and Mary the Warrior-Queen. Enter into the great spiritual struggle. And fight to set things right—not with the puny weapons of the world but with the weapons of the Spirit.

Reflect How can you personally fight for what is right within the Church?

Monday, December 24, 2018

Christmas Eve

LUKE 1:67-79

Zechariah his father, filled with the Holy Spirit, prophesied, saying:

"Blessed be the Lord, the God of Israel;
for he has come to his people and set them free.
He has raised up for us a mighty Savior,
born of the house of his servant David.
Through his prophets he promised of old
that he would save us from our enemies,
from the hands of all who hate us.
He promised to show mercy to our fathers
and to remember his holy covenant.
This was the oath he swore to our father Abraham:
to set us free from the hand of our enemies,
free to worship him without fear,
holy and righteous in his sight
all the days of our life.
You, my child, shall be called the prophet of the Most High,
for you will go before the Lord to prepare his way,
to give his people knowledge of salvation
by the forgiveness of their sins.
In the tender compassion of our God
the dawn from on high shall break upon us,
to shine on those who dwell in darkness and
the shadow of death,
and to guide our feet into the way of peace."

Friends, today's Gospel contains the prayer of Zechariah at the birth of his son, John the Baptist. This prayer is especially precious to priests, religious, and all those who pray the Liturgy of the Hours on a daily basis. It's called the "Benedictus," from its first word in Latin, or the "Canticle of Zechariah."

What's wonderful about this prayer (and why the Church asks its ministers to pray it every day) is that it sums up magnificently the whole history of salvation, putting Jesus and John in the context of the great story of Israel.

John is seen here as the last and greatest of the Old Testament prophets. His role is, like all the prophets, to "go before the Lord to prepare his way." His job is to point, explain, indicate—and then disappear.

Reflect How can you as a Christian act as a prophet in today's secular culture?

Tuesday, December 25, 2018

Nativity *of the* Lord (Christmas)

JOHN 1:1-5, 9-14 [or JOHN 1:1-18]

In the beginning was the Word,
and the Word was with God,
and the Word was God.
He was in the beginning with God.
All things came to be through him,
and without him nothing came to be.
What came to be through him was life,
and this life was the light of the human race;
the light shines in the darkness,
and the darkness has not overcome it.
The true light, which enlightens everyone,
was coming into the world.
He was in the world,
and the world came to be through him,
but the world did not know him.
He came to what was his own,
but his own people did not accept him.

But to those who did accept him
he gave power to become children of God,
to those who believe in his name,
who were born not by natural generation
nor by human choice nor by a man's decision
but of God.

And the Word became flesh
and made his dwelling among us,
and we saw his glory,
the glory as of the Father's only Son,
full of grace and truth.

Friends, today we celebrate the birth of Jesus Christ, the incarnate Son of God.

We hear at Mass one of the most magnificent passages in the Scriptures, indeed one of the gems of the Western literary tradition: the prologue to the Gospel of John. In many ways, the essential meaning of Christmas is contained in these elegantly crafted lines.

But today I would like to focus on two lines in particular. The first is this: "The world came to be through him, but the world did not know him." In that pithily crafted line, we sense the whole tragedy of sin. Human beings were made by and for the Logos and therefore they find their joy in a sort of sympathetic attunement to the Logos. Sin is the disharmony that comes when we fall out of alignment with God's reasonable purpose.

Then comes the incomparably good news: "But to those who did accept him he gave power to become children of God." It is a basic principle of nature that nothing at a lower level of being can rise to a higher level unless it is drawn upward. For example, a plant can become ingredient in a sentient nature only if it is devoured by an animal. By this same principle, a human being can become something higher only when a superior reality assimilates him. The Church Fathers consistently taught that God became human so that humans might become God—which is to say, participants in the divine nature. In a word, we can become children of God precisely because God reached down to us and became a son of man.

Reflect What does it mean to you that God reached down through Christ and made you his very own child, a sharer in the divine nature? How does the Incarnation, God become man, change your view of the value of each human life?

✠

CONCLUSION

Friends,

I'd like to thank you for journeying with me through the Advent season. Now that we've finished, you might be wondering, what's next? How do I maintain the spiritual momentum I developed this Advent? I'd like to suggest a few practical tips.

First, be sure to visit our website, *WordOnFire.org*, on a regular basis. There you'll find lots of helpful resources, including new articles, videos, blog posts, podcasts, and homilies, all designed to help strengthen your faith and evangelize the culture. The best part is that all of it is free!

In addition to those free resources, I invite you to join our new Word on Fire Institute. This is an online hub of deep spiritual and intellectual formation, where you'll journey through courses taught by me and other Fellows. Our goal is to build an army of evangelists, people who have been transformed by Christ and want to bring his light to the world. Learn more and sign up at *https://wordonfire.institute*.

Finally, the best way to carry on your Advent progress is to commit to at least one new spiritual practice. For instance, you might read through one of the Gospels, one chapter per day; or start praying part of the Liturgy of the Hours; or spend some time with the

Blessed Sacrament once a week; or decide to attend one extra Mass each week; or pray one rosary each day, maybe in your car or while you exercise. All of these are simple, straightforward ways to deepen your spiritual life.

Again, thank you from all of us at Word on Fire, and God bless you during this Christmas season!

Peace,

+ Robert Barron

Bishop Robert Barron

Notes:

*Did you enjoy these Advent Gospel Reflections
from Bishop Barron?
We offer FREE Gospel Reflections
delivered to your inbox every day of the year!
Sign up at*
www.DailyCatholicGospel.com